To Andy
Merry Christmas 1995!
Love from
Mumma
:)

Zen
ABC

Illustrated by Amy Zerner and Jessie Spicer Zerner

Charles E. Tuttle Company, Inc.
Boston   Rutland, Vermont   Tokyo

Introduction

Zen is intangible. Its expression is neither verbal nor visual. Yet we seek to experience Zen. We struggle to achieve enlightenment until we understand that to struggle is to become further removed from our goal. . .and when we reach this understanding we can begin to achieve enlightenment. Enlightenment—the experience of no-thing.

Zen ABC is a starting point for parents and their children to begin to share the evocations of Zen experience. We have chosen for each letter of the alphabet a Zen-related word described by a haiku, a koan, or a fragment from the classical literature of Zen. For those unfamiliar, haiku is a special form of Japanese nature poetry. Although traditionally written in three lines with a total of seventeen syllables, contemporary haiku has taken on a freer form while still eliciting an inexpressible meaning. When written by masters such as Bashô and Hô-ô, a Zen haiku is one that causes enhanced perception, so that, as R.H. Blyth puts it, "a haiku is not a poem; it is not literature; it is a hand beckoning, a door half-opened, a mirror wiped clean."[1] A koan also beckons the inquiring mind but its form is the unanswerable question. One of the most famous koans is "what is the sound of one hand clapping?" Koans are used, at times, by Zen masters to test their students; at other times they are a focal point for meditation. They are used here as examples of the multitextured language of Zen.

As stated, every letter has a word; every letter, that is, except X. Instead, there is the story of Hua-yen's returning to the world of delusion—for it is delusion to think that there is a Zen word for the letter X. There is no-thing for X.

Accompanying each letter are the truly exquisite illustrations by Amy Zerner and her mother Jessie Spicer Zerner. This mother-daughter collaboration mirrors the collaboration of words and pictures used in *Zen ABC* to help make accessible the world of Zen.

---

[1]Ernest Wood, *Zen Dictionary* (New York: Philosophical Library, 1957. Reprinted by Charles E. Tuttle Co., 1972), page 49.

wakening

Awakening

Quicksilver whitebait open in the Net
Of Karmic Law their tiny eyes of jet.

— *Bashô*

buddha

Poem for Children

Your mind is Buddha
My mind is also Buddha.
Buddha looks at Buddha;
Mind disappears.
Pine tree shadow reflected on
    the pond is never wet.
Pebble thrown into the water,
Pine tree is dancing.

— *Zen Master Seung Sahn*

 **adence**

Cadence

Spring rain on my roof
  begins to drum:
Drips from the willow, petals
  from the plum.
— *Shôha*

 **ragon Fly**

The Dragon Fly

A stem of grass,
Whereon in vain,
A dragon fly attempts to light.
— *Bashô*

 nlightenment

The geese do not wish to leave their reflection behind;
The water has no mind to retain their image.

 **lower**

The Blue Flower

A flower unknown to bird or
butterfly
Opens its petals: Ah, the
autumn sky!
—*Bashô*

Grace

Chanting a sutra, I am straightway blest:
The morning-glories reach their loveliest.
— *Kyoroku*

aiku

Gigantic Haiku

Down, down, dives the mighty
  Whale:
Higher, higher, rears its lashing
  tail!

—*Buson*

nkin

The Butterfly
Sleeps well
Perched on the
Temple Bell
Till, Clang, it rings.

Joshu's Dog

A monk asked Joshu, a Chinese Zen Master: "Has a dog Buddha-nature or not? Joshu answered: "Mu."

K oan

Ta-sui's Turtle

A monk saw a turtle walking in the garden of Ta-sui's monastery and asked the teacher, "All beings cover their bones with flesh and skin. Why does this being cover its flesh and skin with bones?" Ta-sui, the master, took off one of his sandals and covered the turtle with it.

—*Genro*

 **ove**

The love knot unties
to form a perfect Zen circle
complete in itself.
   —*Lider*

 **editation**

Sitting quietly doing nothing,
Spring comes, grass grows of itself.

 # irvana

This night the Buddha entered Nirvana;
It was like firewood burned utterly away.

One Mind

The One Mind

A hundred gourds: yet they
  have all untwined
Out of a single creeper's
  seed of mind.

     —Chiyo-ni

Pagoda

Topless Tower

Tô-ji Pagoda rises till its
vane
And topmost roof dissolve in
misty rain.
—*Hô-ô*

Quiet

Spring morning—
a goose feather floats
in the quiet room
—*Bruce Ross*

 **eflection**

Soiled Reflection

Under the hazy moon, a
 pool of sky
Is muddied by a frog that
 paddles by.

—*Buson*

Sword

No place for the Sword

A sword! —
Why should one bring such a thing,
Who comes to view the flowers in spring?
—*Kyorai*

ea

In tea the host is simplicity
and the guest elegance
—*Matsudaira Naritada*

Universe

To have the sun and moon in one's sleeve;
To hold the universe in the palm of one's hand.

Voyage

Foam capped wave swells and dies away
sweeping arm erases the voyage.
            —*Lider*

ind

Wind, Steam, and Speed

As wind-waves race across the rice field's sea,
Steam sweeps over my bowl of clear green tea.
—*Hô-ô*

Hua-yen Returns to the World of Delusion

A monk asked Hua-yen, "How does an enlightened person return to the world of delusion?" The master replied, "A broken mirror never reflects again, and the fallen flowers never go back to the old branches."

 **ourself**

Yourself as distinct
and yet as one with all the
creatures, moon and sun.
　　　　—Lider

en

What is Zen?

. . . a fish went to a queen fish and asked: I have always heard about the sea, but what is this sea? Where is it? The queen fish explained: "You live, move, and have your being in the sea. The sea is within you and without you, and you are made of sea, and you will end in sea. The sea surrounds you as your own being."

Published by the Charles E. Tuttle Company, Inc. of
Rutland, Vermont & Tokyo Japan
with editorial offices at
77 Central Street, Boston, Massachusetts 02109.

ISBN 0 8048 1806 1

Credits and Acknowledgments

Every effort has been made to obtain permissions for using the haiku and koans included in *Zen ABC*. The publisher wishes to thank and acknowledge the following for their material:

Sword, Dragon Fly, Inkin (temple bell): *Little Pictures of Japan*, Olive Beaupre Miller, ed., © The Book House for Children, Chicago, 1925.

Enlightenment, Meditation, Nirvana, Universe: *Haiku*, Vol.1, Eastern Culture, © R.H. Blyth, ed., The Hokuseido Press, Tokyo, 1981.

Buddha: *The Whole World Is A Single Flower,* Zen Master Seung Sahn, Charles E. Tuttle Company, Inc., Boston, 1991. © The Providence Zen Center.

Quiet: haiku by Bruce Ross, *Haiku Moment: An Anthology of Contemporary North American Haiku,* © Bruce Ross, ed., Charles E. Tuttle Company, Inc., Boston, forthcoming.

Awakening, Cadence, Grace, Flower, Haiku, One Mind, Pagoda, Reflection, Wind: *A Chime of Windbells,* Harold Stewart, trans., © Charles E. Tuttle Company, Inc., Tokyo, 1969.

Koan, X: *The Iron Flute: 100 Zen Koan*, Nyogen Senzaki, trans. © Charles E. Tuttle Company, Inc., Tokyo, 1964.

Zen: *Zen Flesh, Zen Bones*, Paul Reps, comp. © Charles E. Tuttle Company,Inc., Tokyo, 1957.

Tea: *Cha-No-Yu: The Japanese Tea Ceremony*, A.L. Sadler, © Charles E. Tuttle Company, Inc., Tokyo, 1982.

First printing 1993
Printed in Hong Kong